BECKY GOLDSMITH and LINDA JENKIN

100 Whimsical
APPLIQUÉ DESIGNS

Mix & Match Blocks to Create Playful Quilts
FROM PIECE O' CAKE DESIGNS

C&T PUBLISHING
Another Maker Inspired!

Text copyright © 2023 by Becky Goldsmith and Linda Jenkins

Artwork copyright © 2023 by Becky Goldsmith

Photography © 2023 by C&T Publishing, Inc.

Publisher: Amy Barrett-Daffin

Creative Director: Gailen Runge

Senior Editor: Roxane Cerda

Editor: Liz Aneloski and Gailen Runge

Cover/Book Designer: April Mostek

Production Coordinator: Tim Manibusan

Illustrator: Becky Goldsmith

Photography Coordinator: Rachel Ackley

Photography by C&T Publishing, Inc.

Published by C&T Publishing, Inc., P.O. Box 1456, Lafayette, CA 94549

Library of Congress Cataloging-in-Publication Data

Names: Goldsmith, Becky, 1956- author. | Jenkins, Linda, 1943- author. | Piece O' Cake Designs.

Title: 100 whimsical appliqué designs : mix & match blocks to create playful quilts from Piece O' Cake designs / Becky Goldsmith and Linda Jenkins.

Other titles: One hundred whimsical appliqué designs

Description: Lafayette, CA : C&T Publishing, Another Maker Inspired, [2023] | Summary: "Inside features a collection of 100 whimsical appliqué patterns from Piece O' Cake Designs that can be used in a wide variety of ways; mix and match to make quilts and smaller projects. Quilters can make these appliqué blocks in wool, cotton, or a mix of both using different methods"-- Provided by publisher.

Identifiers: LCCN 2023025727 | ISBN 9781644033135 (trade paperback) | ISBN 9781644033142 (ebook)

Subjects: LCSH: Appliqué--Patterns. | Quilting--Patterns.

Classification: LCC TT779 .G6293 2004 | DDC 746.44/5041--dc23/eng/20230606

LC record available at https://lccn.loc.gov/2023025727

Printed in China

10 9 8 7 6 5 4 3 2 1

Dedication

We dedicate this book to all the quilters who use our books and patterns to make your own cherished quilts.

Acknowledgments

We are forever grateful to our friends at C&T Publishing, who have supported us for the past 20 years. Amazing!

Amy Barrett-Daffin, our publisher, who came up with the idea for this book, is always there when we need her. Liz Aneloski and Gailen Runge, our editors, carefully guided this book to publication. April Mostek, our book designer, put her graphic skills to good use making this book a joy to look at.

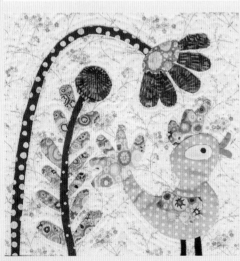

CONTENTS

Introduction

We started Piece O' Cake Designs in 1994 and over the years produced 33 books, 7 blocks of the month, and oh-so-many individual patterns. Inside this book you will find 100 of our favorite whimsical appliqué blocks chosen from these books and patterns.

Combining colors, both prints and solids, in playful ways is one of our greatest joys. The colors that you use in your quilts add flavor and emotion. We encourage you to use colors that make you happy when you make your quilts. You will find yourself smiling as you stitch. :-)

Have fun and happy stitching!
Becky and Linda

Becky & Linda

Copy, Combine, Play!

There are an infinite number of projects to be made using the blocks in this book. Here are a few ideas to get you started:

Enlarge a block to make a one-block quilt (page 16).

Combine several blocks in a multi-block quilt (page 17).

Pair your favorite appliqué blocks with pieced blocks.

Are you working on a quilt that needs an appliqué block? Choose a design from this book!

Embellish a garment with appliqué.

Use the designs for embroidery.

Combine elements from different blocks to make new blocks, as Linda did in her quilt, *Having Fun in the Neighborhood* (page 19).

Turn to the Gallery (pages 16–20) for more ideas. If you like the gallery quilts, they are available for sale individually as downloadable patterns on ctpub.com.

Pay Attention to Scale

The blocks in this book are printed at 8″ × 8″, but many were bigger, or smaller, in their original settings. Intricate designs may look better, and be easier to appliqué, at a larger size. Some may be lovely when reduced in size.

It is important to see the block's finished size before you go too far in the design process. Print, enlarge, or reduce the blocks to the size you want them to be

and then pin them to your design wall. Stand back and evaluate the blocks together. If you need to resize any of them, this is the time to do it.

As you combine different blocks, be sensitive to the way they look together. For example, the bird and flower in Block 52 is out of proportion to the house and tree in Block 91.

But if you enlarge the house Block #91 by 150% and reduce the bird Block #52 by 60%, they fit nicely together. In this example, I put the designs together onto one background to make a new block.

Visual Index of Blocks

Block 1 (page 21)

Block 2 (page 22)

Block 3 (page 23)

Block 4 (page 24)

Block 5 (page 25)

Block 6 (page 26)

Block 7 (page 27)

Block 8 (page 28)

Block 9 (page 29)

Block 10 (page 30)

Block 11 (page 31)

Block 12 (page 32)

Block 13 (page 33)

Block 14 (page 34)

Block 15 (page 35)

Block 16 (page 36)

Block 17 (page 37)

Block 18 (page 38)

Block 19 (page 39)

Block 20 (page 40)

Block 21 (page 41)

Block 22 (page 42)

Block 23 (page 43)

Block 24 (page 44)

Block 25 (page 45)

Block 26 (page 46)

Block 27 (page 47)

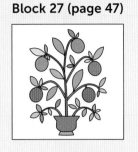

Block 28 (page 48)

Block 29 (page 49)

Block 30 (page 50)

Block 31 (page 51)

Block 32 (page 52)

Block 33 (page 53)

Block 34 (page 54)

Block 35 (page 55)

Block 36 (page 56)

Block 37 (page 57)

Block 38 (page 58)

Block 39 (page 59)

Block 40 (page 60)

Block 41 (page 61)

Block 42 (page 62)

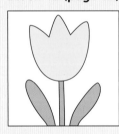

Block 43 (page 63)

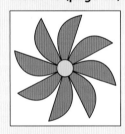

Block 44 (page 64)

Block 45 (page 65)

Block 46 (page 66)

Block 47 (page 67)

Block 48 (page 68)

Block 49 (page 69)

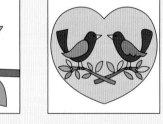

Block 50 (page 70)

Block 51 (page 71)

Block 52 (page 72)

Block 53 (page 73)

Block 54 (page 74)

Block 55 (page 75)

Block 56 (page 76)

Block 57 (page 77)

Block 58 (page 78)

Block 59 (page 79)

Block 60 (page 80)

Block 61 (page 82)

Block 62 (page 84)

Block 63 (page 86)

Block 64 (page 87)

Block 65 (page 88)

Block 66 (page 89)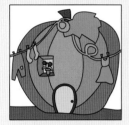

Block 67 (page 90)

Block 68 (page 91)

Block 69 (page 92)

Block 70 (page 93)

Block 71 (page 94)

Block 72 (page 95)

Block 73 (page 96)

Block 74 (page 97)

Block 75 (page 98)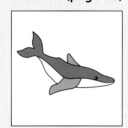

Block 76 (page 99)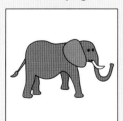

Block 77 (page 100)

Block 78 (page 101)

Block 79 (page 102)

Block 80 (page 103)

Block 81 (page 104)

Block 82 (page 105)

Block 83 (page 106)

Block 84 (page 107)

Block 85 (page 108)

Block 86 (page 109)

Block 87 (page 110)

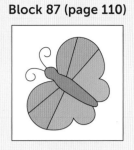

Block 88 (page 111)

Block 89 (page 112)

Block 90 (page 113)

Block 91 (page 114)

Block 92 (page 115)

Block 93 (page 116)

Block 94 (page 117)

Block 95 (page 118)

Block 96 (page 119)

Block 97 (page 120)

Block 98 (page 121)

Block 99 (page 122)

Block 100 (page 123)

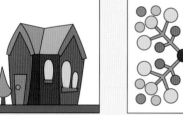

Border 101 (page 124)

Border 102 (page 125)

Border 103 (page 126)

Border 104 (page 127)

General Instructions

How to use the patterns

Look through the Visual Index (pages 7–10) to find blocks that interest you. Make a copy of the block patterns and pin them to your design wall.

Consider any other elements you will use with the appliqué blocks such as sashing, pieced blocks, borders, etc. Decide on the finished sizes of all elements as well as the finished size of your quilt.

Refer to the Reduction/Enlargement Table (below) and reduce or enlarge the appliqué blocks as needed. Trim and/or tape pages together to make a finished size pattern for the appliqué blocks and borders. Place the finished size patterns on your design wall and give them a good look before moving on.

REDUCTION/ENLARGEMENT TABLE

Enlarge or reduce blocks by the percentage in the Reducing and Enlarging table (at right) to make a pattern in the desired size.

If your copy machine will only enlarge 200% (creating a 16˝ block), and you want a larger block, you can enlarge in two or three stages. For blocks 17˝ to 32˝, first enlarge the 8˝ block 200% to create a 16˝ block. Then enlarge again using the Two-Stage Enlarging table at right. If you want a block 33˝ to 48˝, first enlarge the 8˝ block 200% to create a 16˝ block, then enlarge 200% again to create a 32˝ block. Then enlarge again using the Three-Stage Enlarging table at right.

Two important notes for larger blocks:

- Putting together the larger tiled blocks can be a bit of a challenge. Keep in mind you can always take advantage of large-format printers at many copy shops.

- The pattern lines on the printout will get thicker. Follow the advice on page 14 to split the line with your scissors when you are cutting out the shapes.

ONE-STAGE REDUCING AND ENLARGING

New size*	%	New size*	%
4˝	50%	27˝	338%
5˝	63%	28˝	350%
6˝	75%	29˝	363%
7˝	88%	30˝	375%
8˝	100%	31˝	388%
9˝	113%	32˝	400%
10˝	125%	33˝	413%
11˝	138%	34˝	425%
12˝	150%	35˝	438%
13˝	163%	36˝	450%
14˝	175%	37˝	463%
15˝	188%	38˝	475%
16˝	200%	39˝	488%
17˝	213%	40˝	500%
18˝	225%	41˝	513%
19˝	238%	42˝	525%
20˝	250%	43˝	538%
21˝	263%	44˝	550%
22˝	275%	45˝	563%
23˝	288%	46˝	575%
24˝	300%	47˝	588%
25˝	313%	48˝	600%
26˝	325%		

* Original block size 8˝

TWO-STAGE ENLARGING

New size*	%	New size*	%
17˝	106%	26˝	163%
18˝	113%	27˝	169%
19˝	119%	28˝	175%
20˝	125%	29˝	181%
21˝	131%	30˝	188%
22˝	138%	31˝	194%
23˝	144%	32˝	200%
24˝	150%		
25˝	156%		

* Original block size 16˝ (having enlarged 8˝ block by 200%)

THREE-STAGE ENLARGING

New size*	%	New size*	%
33˝	103%	42˝	131%
34˝	106%	43˝	134%
35˝	109%	44˝	138%
36˝	113%	45˝	141%
37˝	116%	46˝	144%
38˝	119%	47˝	147%
39˝	122%	48˝	150%
40˝	125%		
41˝	128%		

* Original block size 32˝ (having enlarged 8˝ block by 200% twice)

Yardage Table

If you are using the same backing fabric for multiple blocks, you can use the yardage chart to determine how much yardage you'll need. When using the chart, keep in mind it is based on 40"-wide fabric. If your fabric is wider, you might need less fabric. The chart also adds 1/8 yard to the measurements, which will allow for potential shrinking if you wash the fabric and to straighten out the edge before cutting. You might want to purchase more fabric, particularly if you need many strips, in case you cut a strip inaccurately.

The chart takes you up to 18" finished blocks, which require 20" × 20" background squares. Beyond 20", you'll only fit one block per strip (for 40" fabric). Multiply the background cut size by the number of blocks you need and divide by 36" to calculate your yardage.

BACKGROUND YARDAGE

Block size	Background size	# of blocks	Yardage needed
6"	8"	1–5	3/8
6"	8"	6–10	5/8
6"	8"	11–15	7/8
6"	8"	16–20	1 1/8
6"	8"	21–25	1 1/4
6"	8"	26–30	1 1/2
6"	8"	31–35	1 3/4
6"	8"	36–40	2
6"	8"	41–45	2 1/8
7"	9"	1–4	3/8
7"	9"	5–8	5/8
7"	9"	9–12	7/8
7"	9"	13–16	1 1/8
7"	9"	17–20	1 3/8
7"	9"	21–24	1 5/8
7"	9"	25–28	1 7/8
7"	9"	29–32	2 1/8
7"	9"	33–36	2 3/8
7"	9"	37–40	2 5/8
7"	9"	41–44	2 7/8
7"	9"	45–48	3 1/8
8"	10"	1–4	1/2
8"	10"	5–8	3/4
8"	10"	9–12	1
8"	10"	13–16	1 1/4
8"	10"	17–20	1 5/8
8"	10"	21–24	1 7/8
8"	10"	25–28	2 1/8
8"	10"	29–32	2 3/8
8"	10"	33–36	2 5/8
8"	10"	37–40	3
8"	10"	41–44	3 1/4
8"	10"	45–48	3 1/2
9"	11"	1–3	1/2
9"	11"	4–6	3/4
9"	11"	7–9	1 1/8
9"	11"	10–12	1 3/8
9"	11"	13–15	1 2/3
9"	11"	16–18	2
9"	11"	19–21	2 1/3
9"	11"	22–24	2 5/8
9"	11"	25–27	2 7/8
9"	11"	28–30	3 1/4
9"	11"	31–33	3 1/2
9"	11"	34–36	3 7/8
9"	11"	37–39	4 1/8
9"	11"	40–42	4 1/2
9"	11"	43–45	4 3/4
10"	12"	1–3	1/2
10"	12"	4–6	7/8
10"	12"	7–9	1 1/8
10"	12"	10–12	1 1/2
10"	12"	13–15	1 7/8
10"	12"	16–18	2 1/8
10"	12"	19–21	2 1/2
10"	12"	22–24	2 7/8
10"	12"	25–27	3 1/8
10"	12"	28–30	3 1/2
10"	12"	31–33	3 7/8
10"	12"	34–36	4 1/8
10"	12"	37–39	4 1/2
10"	12"	40–42	4 7/8
10"	12"	43–45	5 1/8
11"	13"	1–3	1/2
11"	13"	4–6	7/8
11"	13"	7–9	1 1/4
11"	13"	10–12	1 5/8
11"	13"	13–15	2
11"	13"	16–18	2 1/3
11"	13"	19–21	2 2/3
11"	13"	22–24	3 1/8
11"	13"	25–27	3 3/8
11"	13"	28–30	3 3/4
11"	13"	31–33	4 1/8
11"	13"	34–36	4 1/2
11"	13"	37–39	4 7/8
11"	13"	40–42	5 1/4
11"	13"	43–45	5 5/8
12"	14"	1–2	5/8
12"	14"	3–4	1
12"	14"	5–6	1 1/3
12"	14"	7–8	1 3/4
12"	14"	9–10	2 1/8
12"	14"	11–12	2 1/2
12"	14"	13–14	2 7/8
12"	14"	15–16	3 1/4
12"	14"	17–18	3 5/8
12"	14"	19–20	4 1/8
12"	14"	21–22	4 1/2
12"	14"	23–24	4 7/8
12"	14"	25–26	5 1/4
12"	14"	27–28	5 5/8
12"	14"	29–30	6
12"	14"	31–32	6 3/8
12"	14"	33–34	6 3/4
12"	14"	35–36	7 1/8
12"	14"	37–38	7 5/8
12"	14"	39–40	8
12"	14"	41–42	8 1/3

Block size	Background size	# of blocks	Yardage needed
13″	15″	1–2	5/8
13″	15″	3–4	1
13″	15″	5–6	1 3/8
13″	15″	7–8	1 7/8
13″	15″	9–10	2 1/4
13″	15″	11–12	2 5/8
13″	15″	13–14	3 1/8
13″	15″	15–16	3 1/2
13″	15″	17–18	3 7/8
13″	15″	19–20	4 1/3
13″	15″	21–22	4 3/4
13″	15″	23–24	5 1/8
13″	15″	25–26	5 5/8
13″	15″	27–28	6
13″	15″	29–30	6 1/2
13″	15″	31–32	6 7/8
13″	15″	33–34	7 1/4
13″	15″	35–36	7 5/8
13″	15″	37–38	8 1/8
13″	15″	39–40	8 1/2
13″	15″	41–42	8 7/8
14″	16″	1–2	5/8
14″	16″	3–4	1
14″	16″	5–6	1 1/2
14″	16″	7–8	2
14″	16″	9–10	2 3/8
14″	16″	11–12	2 7/8
14″	16″	13–14	3 1/4
14″	16″	15–16	3 3/4
14″	16″	17–18	4 1/8
14″	16″	19–20	4 5/8
14″	16″	21–22	5 1/8
14″	16″	23–24	5 1/2
14″	16″	25–26	6
14″	16″	27–28	6 3/8
14″	16″	29–30	6 7/8
14″	16″	31–32	7 1/4
14″	16″	33–34	7 3/4
14″	16″	35–36	8 1/8
14″	16″	37–38	8 5/8
14″	16″	39–40	9 1/8
14″	16″	41–42	9 1/2

Block size	Background size	# of blocks	Yardage needed
15″	17″	1–2	5/8
15″	17″	3–4	1 1/8
15″	17″	5–6	1 5/8
15″	17″	7–8	2 1/8
15″	17″	9–10	2 1/2
15″	17″	11–12	3
15″	17″	13–14	3 1/2
15″	17″	15–16	4
15″	17″	17–18	4 3/8
15″	17″	19–20	4 7/8
15″	17″	21–22	5 1/3
15″	17″	23–24	5 7/8
15″	17″	25–26	6 1/3
15″	17″	27–28	6 3/4
15″	17″	29–30	7 1/4
15″	17″	31–32	7 3/4
15″	17″	33–34	8 1/4
15″	17″	35–36	8 5/8
15″	17″	37–38	9 1/8
15″	17″	39–40	9 5/8
15″	17″	41–42	10 1/8
16″	18″	1–2	5/8
16″	18″	3–4	1 1/8
16″	18″	5–6	1 5/8
16″	18″	7–8	2 1/8
16″	18″	9–10	2 5/8
16″	18″	11–12	3 1/8
16″	18″	13–14	3 5/8
16″	18″	15–16	4 1/8
16″	18″	17–18	4 5/8
16″	18″	19–20	5 1/8
16″	18″	21–22	5 5/8
16″	18″	23–24	6 1/8
16″	18″	25–26	6 5/8
16″	18″	27–28	7
16″	18″	29–30	7 5/8
16″	18″	31–32	8 1/8
16″	18″	33–34	8 5/8
16″	18″	35–36	9 1/8
16″	18″	37–38	9 5/8
16″	18″	39–40	10 1/8
16″	18″	41–42	10 5/8

Block size	Background size	# of blocks	Yardage needed
17″	19″	1–2	2/3
17″	19″	3–4	1 1/4
17″	19″	5–6	1 3/4
17″	19″	7–8	2 1/4
17″	19″	9–10	2 7/8
17″	19″	11–12	3 1/3
17″	19″	13–14	4
17″	19″	15–16	4 3/8
17″	19″	17–18	4 7/8
17″	19″	19–20	5 1/2
17″	19″	21–22	6
17″	19″	23–24	6 1/8
17″	19″	25–26	7
17″	19″	27–28	7 5/8
17″	19″	29–30	8 1/8
17″	19″	31–32	8 5/8
17″	19″	33–34	9 1/8
17″	19″	35–36	9 5/8
17″	19″	37–38	10 1/4
17″	19″	39–40	10 3/4
17″	19″	41–42	11 1/4
18″	20″	1–2	3/4
18″	20″	3–4	1 1/4
18″	20″	5–6	1 7/8
18″	20″	7–8	2 3/8
18″	20″	9–10	3
18″	20″	11–12	3 1/2
18″	20″	13–14	4 1/8
18″	20″	15–16	4 5/8
18″	20″	17–18	5 1/8
18″	20″	19–20	5 3/4
18″	20″	21–22	6 1/4
18″	20″	23–24	6 7/8
18″	20″	25–26	7 3/8
18″	20″	27–28	8
18″	20″	29–30	8 1/2
18″	20″	31–32	9 1/8
18″	20″	33–34	9 5/8
18″	20″	35–36	10 1/8
18″	20″	37–38	10 3/4
18″	20″	39–40	11 1/4
18″	20″	41–42	11 7/8

Appliqué Instructions

Refer to the book, *The Best-Ever Appliqué Sampler,* by Becky Goldsmith and Linda Jenkins (C&T Publishing), and/or *Hand Sewing,* by Becky Goldsmith (C&T Publishing), for more detailed appliqué instructions.

TEMPLATES

Appliqué templates are the finished size of the shape—no seam allowances are added. Keep the shapes for each block together. Each appliqué shape requires its own template. When shapes overlap, you will need a template for each of those shapes.

1. Make 2–3 copies of each finished size block onto plain paper, *English Paper-Piecing Specialty Paper* (C&T Publishing), or white card stock. Choose which shapes will be cut out from each copied sheet.

2. Cover the template shapes with a single-sided self-adhesive laminating sheet, available at an office supply store.

3. Cut out each template, splitting the drawn line with your scissors. Do not cut outside of the lines as it adds to the size of the template. Keep edges smooth and points sharp.

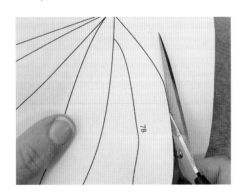

MAKE A PLACEMENT OVERLAY

The placement overlay allows you to accurately position your shapes on the block without tracing on your background fabric or the need to use a lightbox.

1. Cut a piece of clear, medium-weight vinyl, such as *Premium Clear Vinyl* (C&T Publishing), to the finished size of the block.

2. Tape the pattern onto a table to keep it from shifting out of place. Tape the vinyl over the pattern.

3. Use a black ultra fine point permanent marker (we use Sharpie Ultra Fine Point marker) to draw the horizontal and vertical center lines onto the vinyl. Draw an "X" in the upper right-hand corner of the overlay.

4. Trace the pattern and the numbers onto the vinyl. If your pen goes off the line, just pick it up and move it back in place. You won't be graded on how well you trace :-).

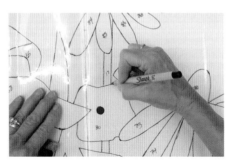

PREPARE THE BACKGROUND BLOCKS

1. Add 1˝ to each side of the finished size of the block and cut backgrounds this size. For example, you would cut the background 12˝ × 12˝ for a 10˝ × 10˝ finished size block.

2. Press the block and border backgrounds in half, horizontally and vertically. The pressed-in grid aligns with the drawn center grid on the placement overlay.

3. Draw a short line on each end of the pressed-in lines at the raw edges of the fabric. These short lines help when you position the placement overlay on the block.

4. Draw an "X" in the far upper right-hand corner of the background in the excess fabric that will be trimmed away after your appliqué is complete.

USE THE PLACEMENT OVERLAY TO POSITION APPLIQUÉ SHAPES

1. Place the block right side up on your sandboard, cutting mat, or ironing surface if you are fusing.

2. Place the overlay right side up over the block, lining up the centerlines, with the corner Xs aligned.

3. Hold the overlay in place with one hand. Lift the edge of overlay and slide the appliqué shape into place. Adjust as needed and then pin, or fuse, the shape in place.

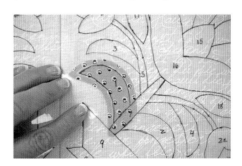

Stitching Options

Choose your favorite appliqué method. You can combine methods to fit your needs. Refer to the book, *The Best-Ever Appliqué Sampler*, by Becky Goldsmith and Linda Jenkins, and/or *Hand Sewing*, by Becky Goldsmith, for more detailed appliqué instructions.

NEEDLE-TURN HAND APPLIQUÉ

Place your appliqué fabric right side up on a sandboard to keep the fabric from shifting. Place your template right side up on the fabric and trace around it. Cut shapes out adding a ³⁄₁₆˝ seam allowance.

Finger-press the seam allowance to the back of the appliqué shapes before placing them on the block. You'll be amazed at how much easier this one step makes turning the seam allowance under.

Use the placement overlay to position shapes on the background. Pin or baste and then stitch them in place.

FUSIBLE APPLIQUÉ

Follow the directions on the package of fusible web. Use a Teflon pressing sheet to protect the iron and the ironing surface. Do not overheat the fusible.

Raw edges can be finished by hand or machine with a blanket stitch, satin stitch, or any stitch that suits you.

WOOL APPLIQUÉ

Felted wool and wool felt are lovely to appliqué with. We use SoftFuse fusible web to hold wool shapes in place on the block and to help stabilize the raw edges. You can also use pins, some glues, or basting.

Sew the edges of the appliqué with a whip stitch or blanket stitch. Wool thread in matching colors is more invisible. Perle cotton is showier depending on thread weight and color.

Wool appliqué looks great with embroidery—a little or a lot :-).

EMBROIDER THE BLOCKS

Use a lightbox and trace the block design onto your background fabric. Embroider the outlines and fill the shapes with stitches of your choice. You can use one color, like red or blue, or use a variety of colors.

You can also combine hand-sewn or fused appliqué shapes with embroidered areas!

Quilt Assembly and Finishing

ASSEMBLE THE QUILT TOP

1. Press appliqué blocks and borders.

2. Use rotary tools and trim blocks, being sure to add ½˝ to the finished size for the seam allowances.

3. Place all the blocks and borders in position on your design wall. Take a photograph of your quilt for reference.

4. Sew the quilt together in rows. Press the seam allowances to one side, in opposite directions so that they nest when rows are sewn together.

5. Sew rows together. Press seam allowances in the direction they lay flattest.

LAYER, BASTE, AND QUILT

1. Layer the quilt back, batting, and quilt top. Be sure layers are centered and smooth.

2. Baste the layers together.

3. Quilt by hand or machine.

Finish the Quilt

You are almost done! Finish the outer edges with binding. Add a hanging sleeve and documentation patch. Add a final flourish by signing the front or back of your quilt with a permanent pen or embroidery.

Inspiration/Gallery

Blocks combined to make new and different quilts! The patterns
for these quilts are available on the C&T Website, ctpub.com.

Fresh from the Garden *Made by Linda Jenkins*

FINISHED QUILT: 42½″ × 55″

To make this quilt, we enlarged Block 23 by 675%. At this scale, it makes an impressive wall quilt!

Birds of a Feather *Made by Linda Jenkins*

FINISHED QUILT: 37½″ × 37½″ • BLOCKS: 10″ × 10″ • SASHING SQUARES: 1″ × 1″

INNER BORDERS: 1″-wide • OUTER BORDERS: 6¼″-wide

This quilt is a combination of Blocks 50, 52, 53, and 55 and Border Block 104.

The four bird blocks are originally from our book, *Whimsical Quilt Garden*.
The border was originally in our book, *Aunt Millie's Garden*. They are perfect together in this quilt.

Flutterbye, Butterflies *Made by Becky Goldsmith*

FINISHED QUILT: 40˝ × 40˝ • BUTTERFLY BLOCK: 8˝ × 8˝ • VINE BORDER: 4˝-wide

This quilt is a combination of Butterfly Block 88 and the Vine Border 102.
The heart in one corner of each Butterfly Block is optional. Becky liked the way they came
together at the center of the quilt and only stitched them to the four center blocks.

Having Fun in the Neighborhood *Made by Linda Jenkins*

FINISHED QUILT: 29˝ × 53˝ • FINISHED BLOCK: 24˝ × 48˝

INNER BORDER: 1˝-wide • OUTER BORDER: 1½˝-wide

This quilt is a combination of Block 61 and Block 66.
Linda mixed and matched elements from both blocks
to make this one, very cute quilt!

Block 66, with the pumpkin, was enlarged 150%.
Block 61 was enlarged 275%.

These blocks were originally published in two different books,
Rhymes I Remember and *Covered with Love.*

O Happy Day! *Made by Becky Goldsmith*

FINISHED QUILT: 48˝ x 48˝ • ROOSTER BLOCK: 30˝ x 30˝

SASHING: 1˝-wide • LEAF BLOCKS: 4˝ x 8˝

This quilt is a combination of Block 57 and Border 103.

The Rooster block has been enlarged by 375% to an impressive size of 30˝ x 30˝.
This happy fellow, surrounded by the leaves in the border, is perfect for the wall
or as a small quilt to cuddle up under.

Block 1

Block 2

Block 3

Block 4

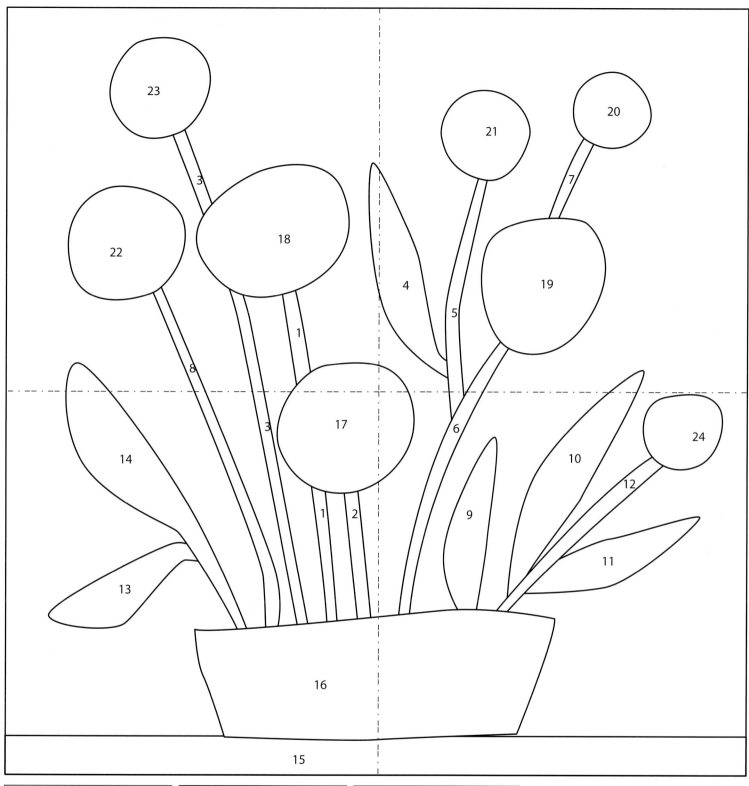

Block 5

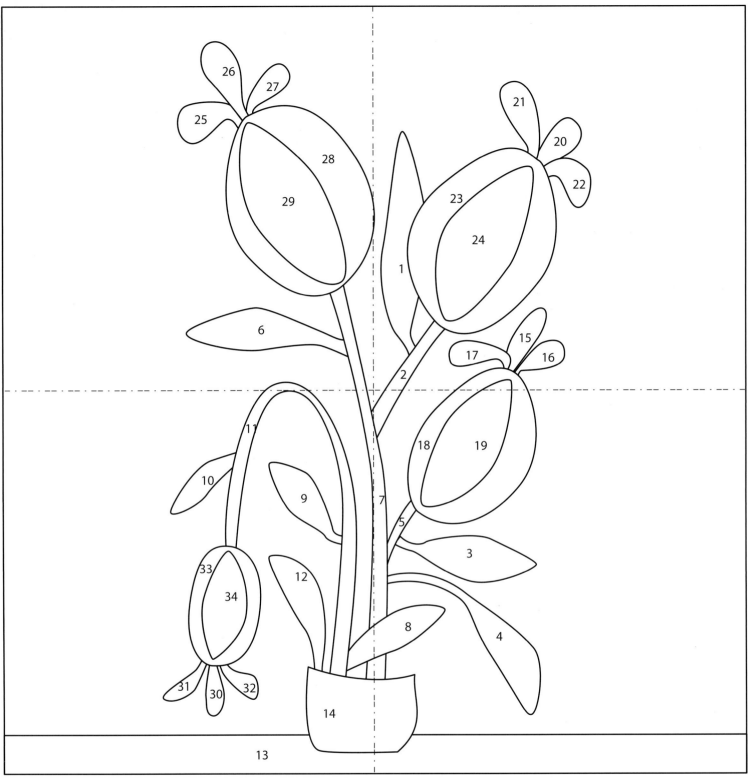

Block 6

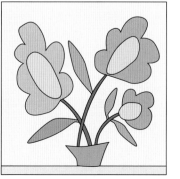

Block 7

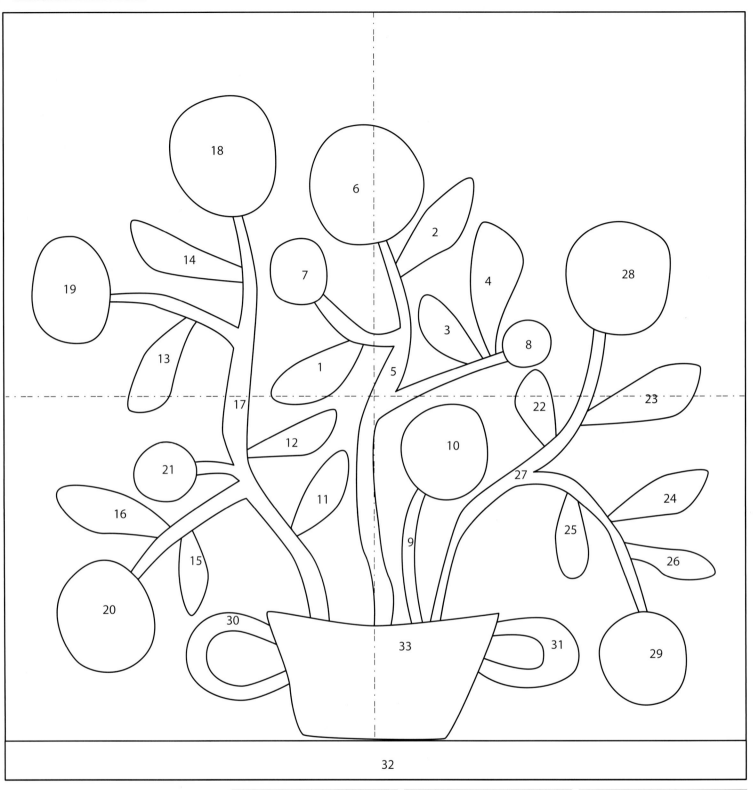

Block 8

Block 9

Block 10

Block 11

Block 12

Block 13

Block 14

Block 15

Block 16

Block 17

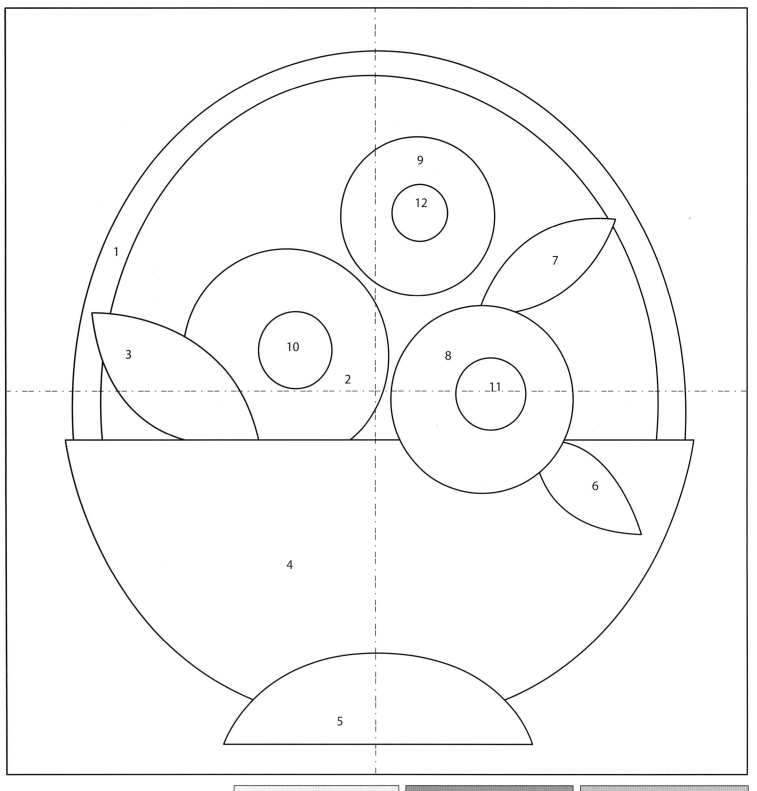

Block 18

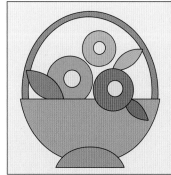 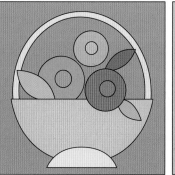 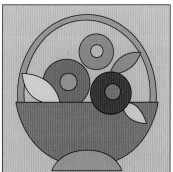

Block 19

Block 20

Block 21

Block 22

Block 23

Block 24

Block 25

Block 26

Block 27

Block 28

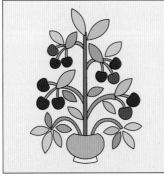

Block 29

Block 30

Block 31

Block 32

Block 33

Block 34

Block 35

Block 36

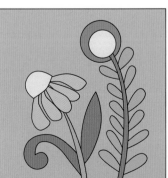

Block 37

Block 38

Block 39

Block 40

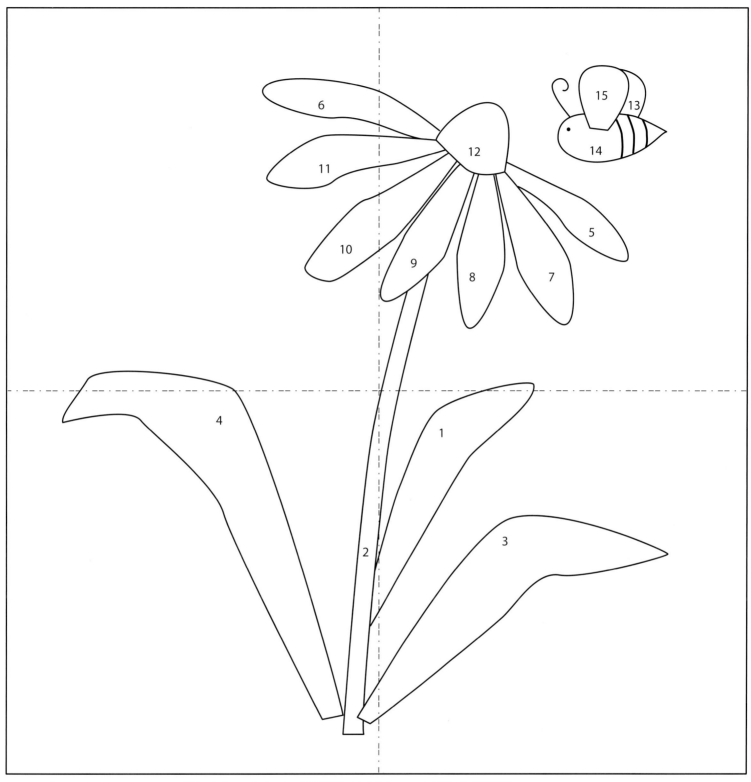

Block 41

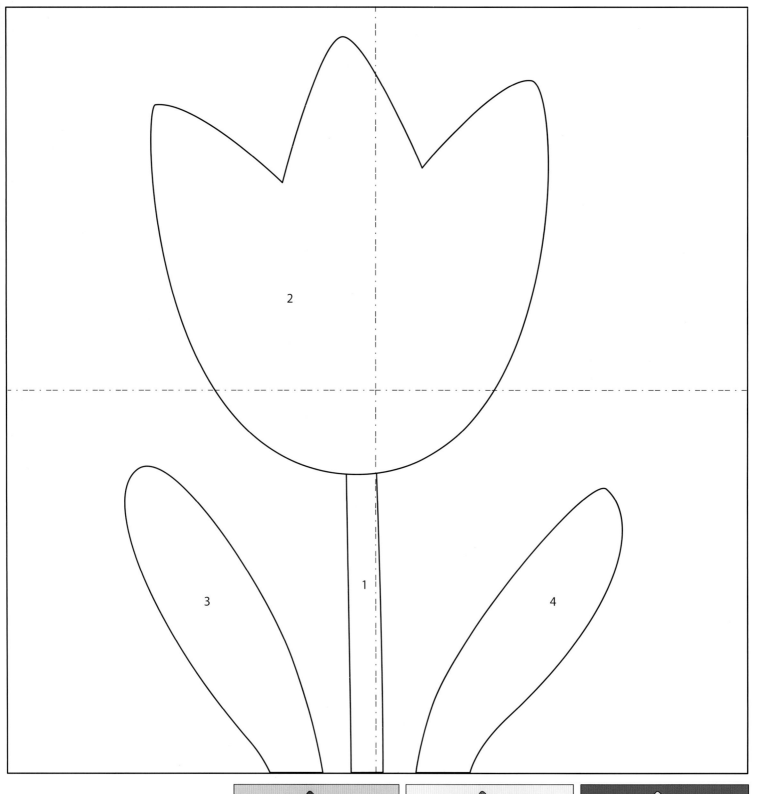

Block 42

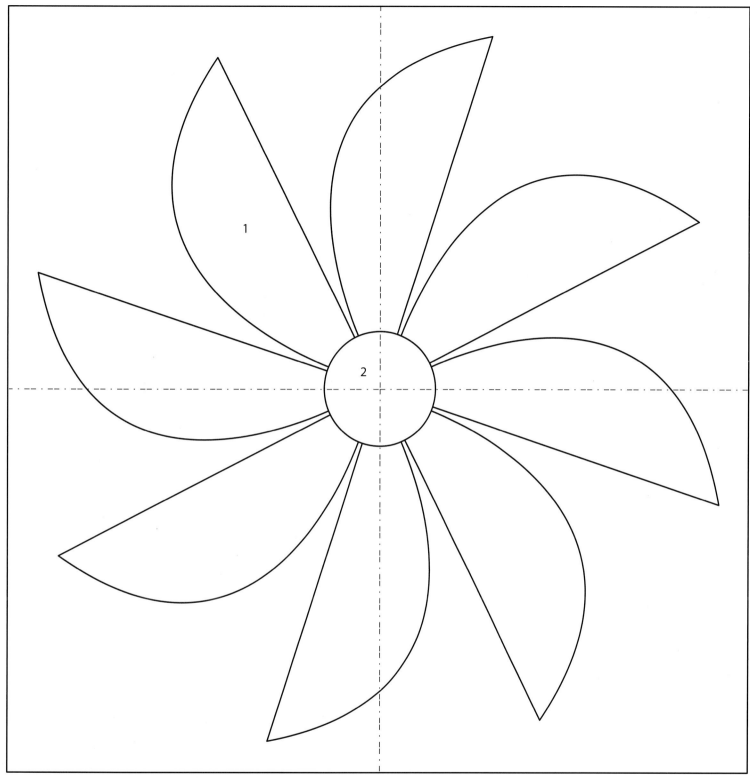

1

2

Block 43

Block 44

Block 45

Block 46

Block 47

Block 48

Block 49

Block 50

Block 51

Block 52

Block 53

Block 54

Block 55

Block 56

Block 57

Block 58

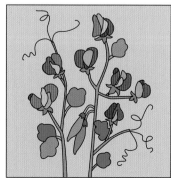

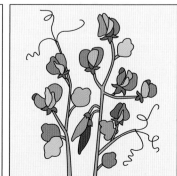

Block 59

34

11

4

22

18

8

9

10

19 21

5 7

17

1

20

6

45

46 44

47 43

42

41 40

33

30

30 32

38 37

31

31

3

24

23

39

2

Block 60a

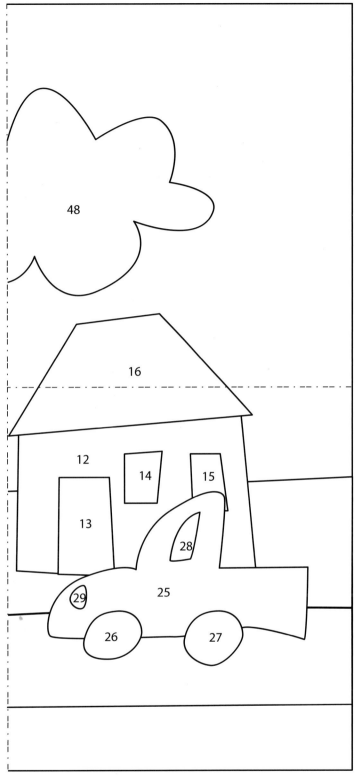

48

16

12

14

15

13

28

25

29

26

27

Block 60b

Block 61a

Block 61b

Block 62

Block 63

Block 64

19

21

20

5

4

3

10

11

12

9

8

6

7

13

15/16

14

15/16

1

2

17

18

Block 65

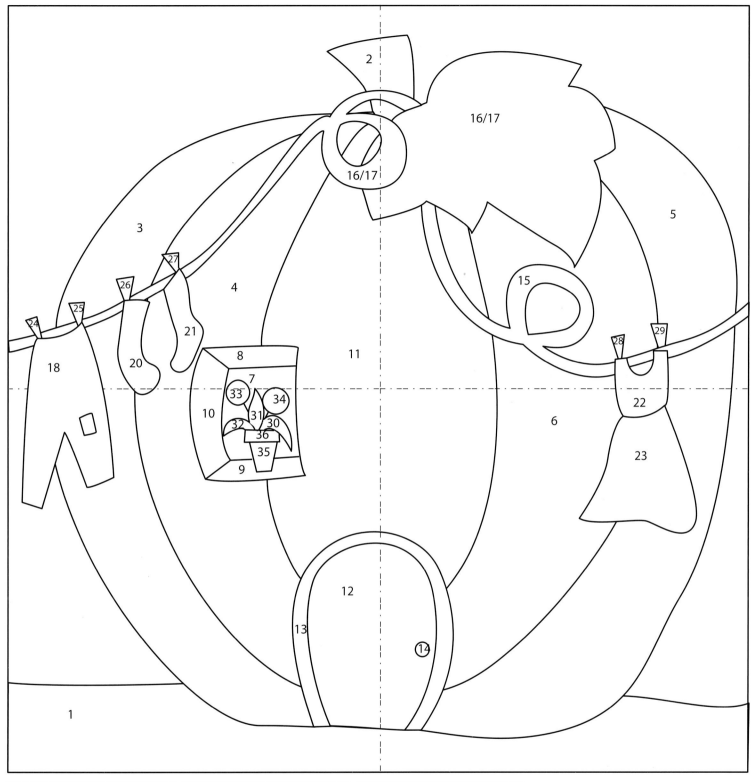

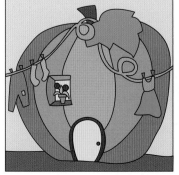
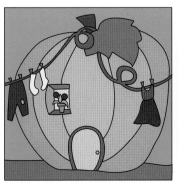
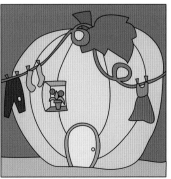

Block 66

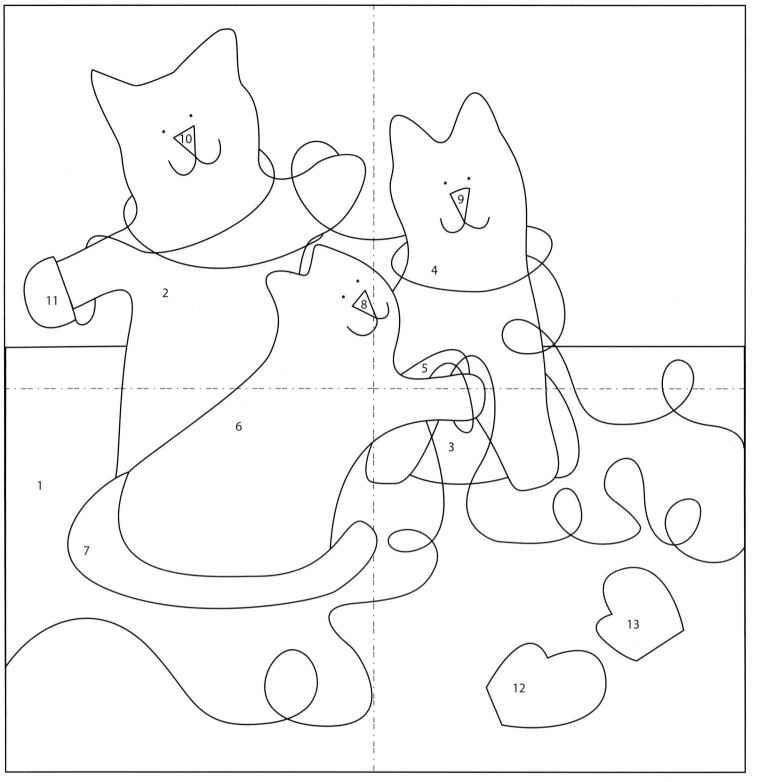

Block 67

Block 68

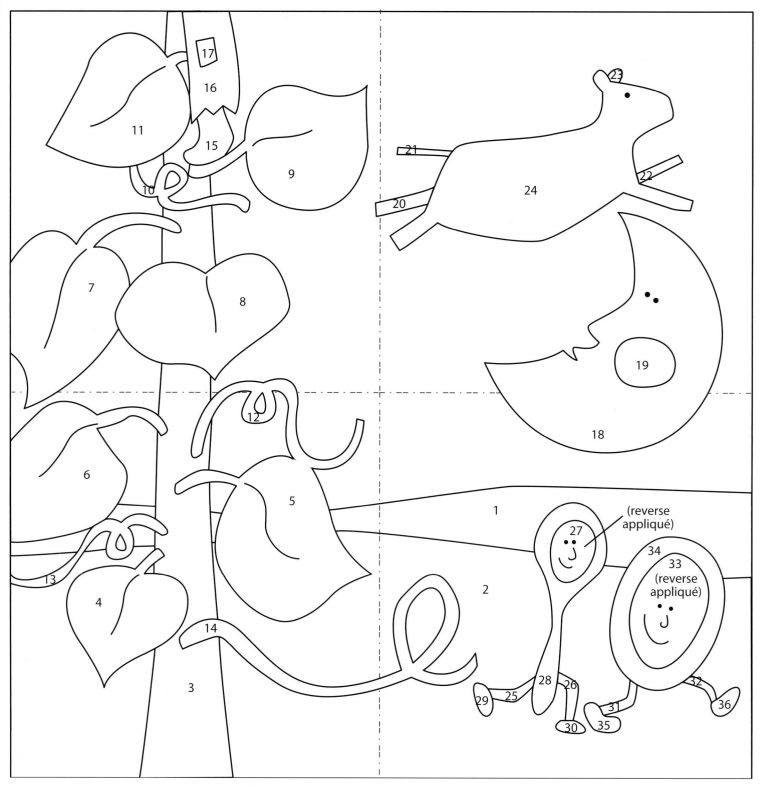

Block 69

7

11 12

3

9

10

5

6

4

8 TEA

2

1

Block 70

Block 71

Block 72

Block 73

Block 74

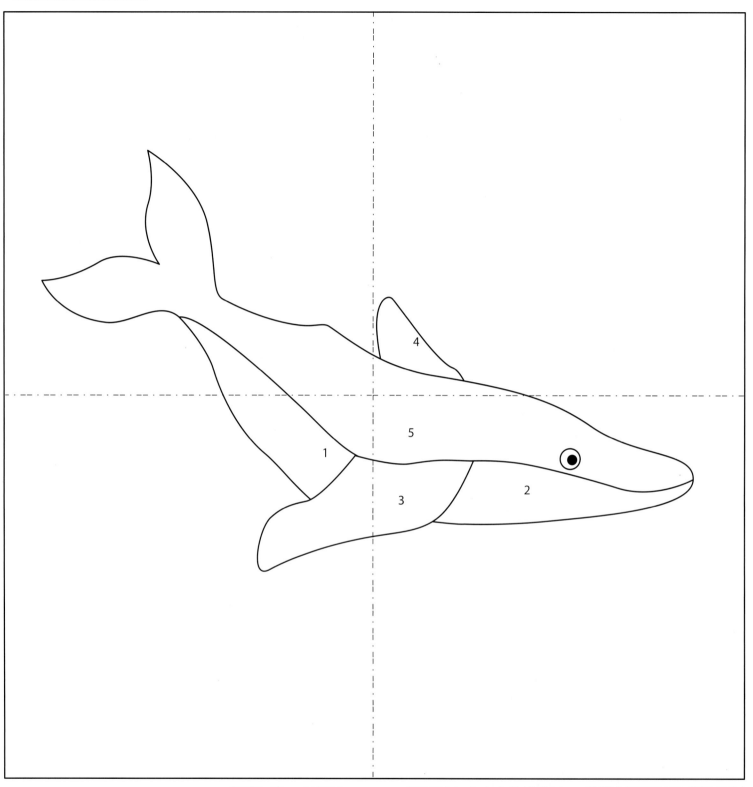

Block 75

Block 76

Block 77

Block 78

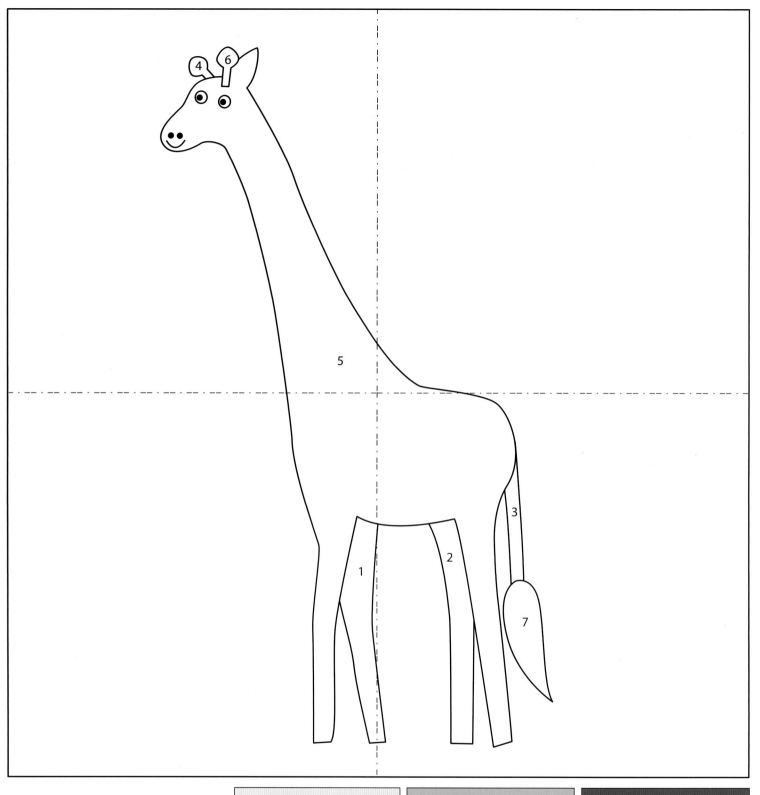

Block 79

2

1

Block 80

Block 81

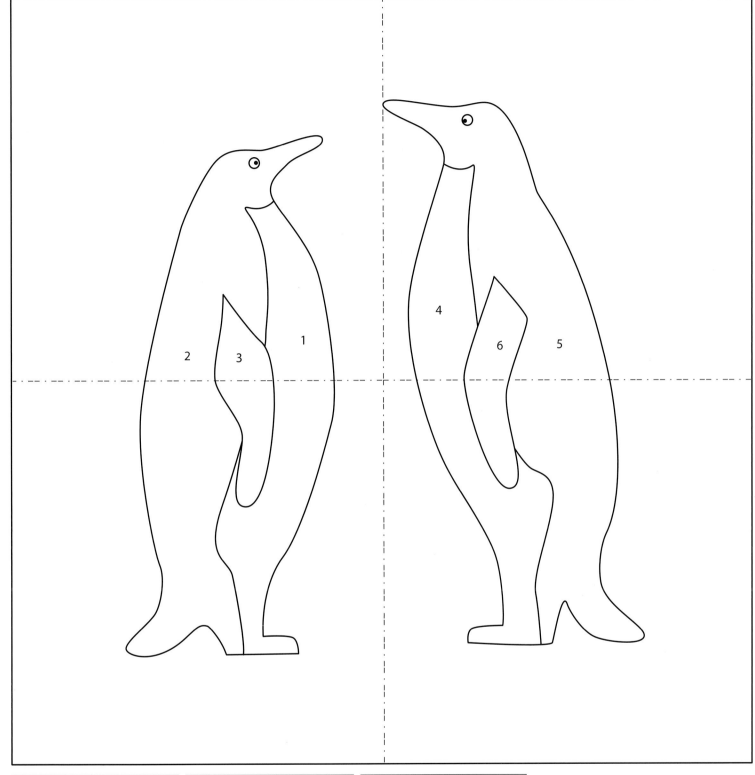

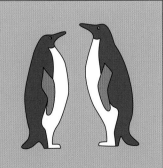

Block 82

Block 83

Block 84

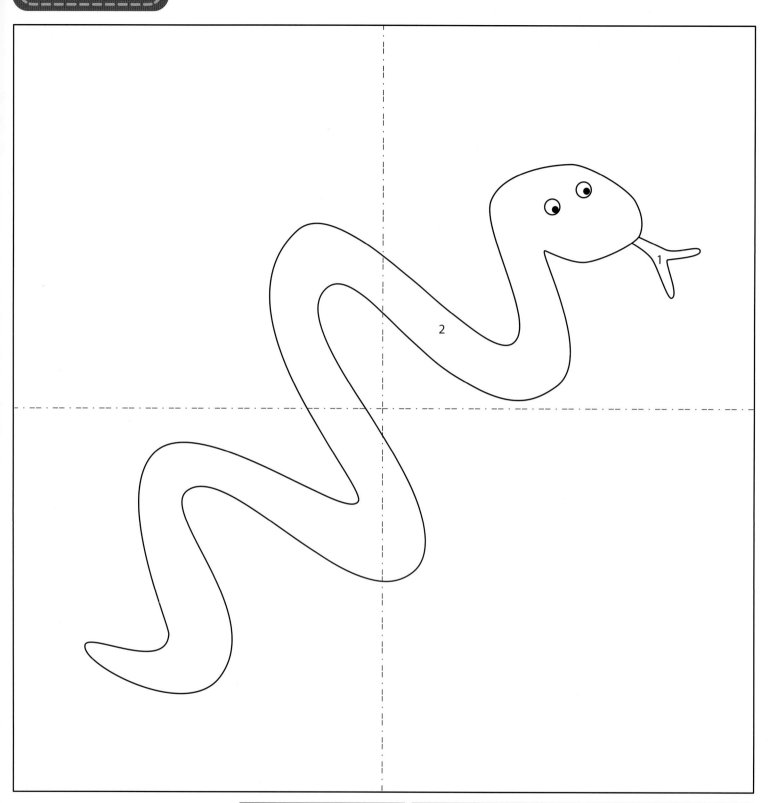

1

2

Block 85

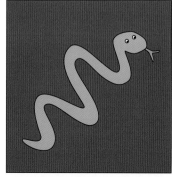
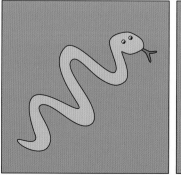

Block 86

Block 87

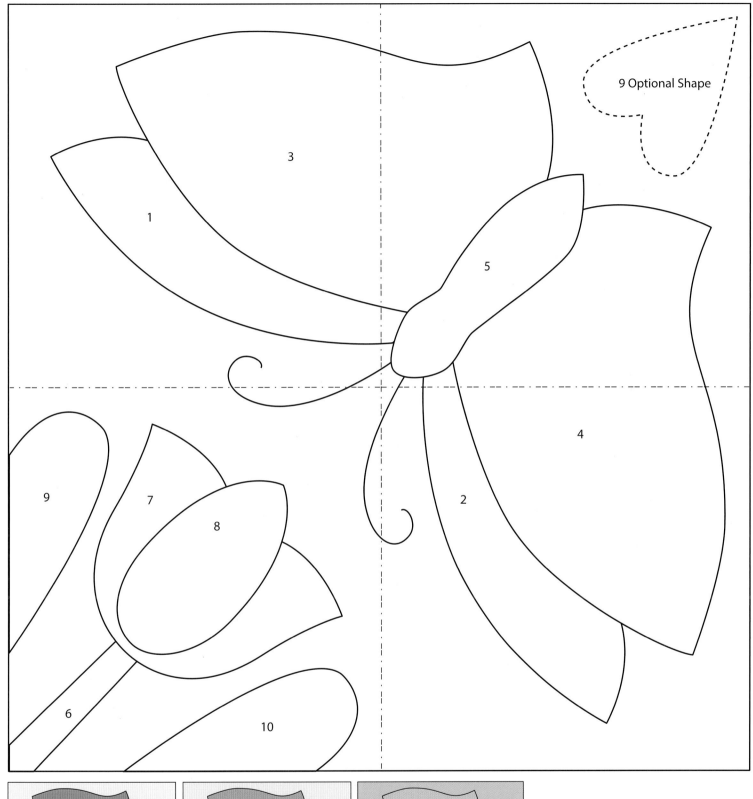

9 Optional Shape

3

1

5

4

2

9

7

8

6

10

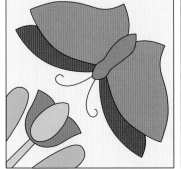  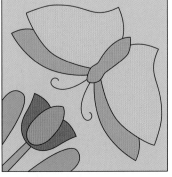

Block 88

Shapes 5-8 are optional

Block 89

7

9

8

6

5

4

3

1

2

Optional flower embroidery.

Block 90

10

8

18

12

13
(reverse
appliqué)

11

14

3

17

9

9

4
(reverse
appliqué)

5

2
(reverse
appliqué)

16

1
(reverse
appliqué)

6

7

15

19

Block 91

all leaves
11

10

9

5

3
(reverse
appliqué)

2

4
(reverse
appliqué)

6

1

7

8

12

Block 92

18

14

17

12

13

16

11
(reverse applique)

15

4

3
(reverse applique)

8

9

10

5

6

7

1
(reverse applique)

2
(reverse applique)

19

Block 93

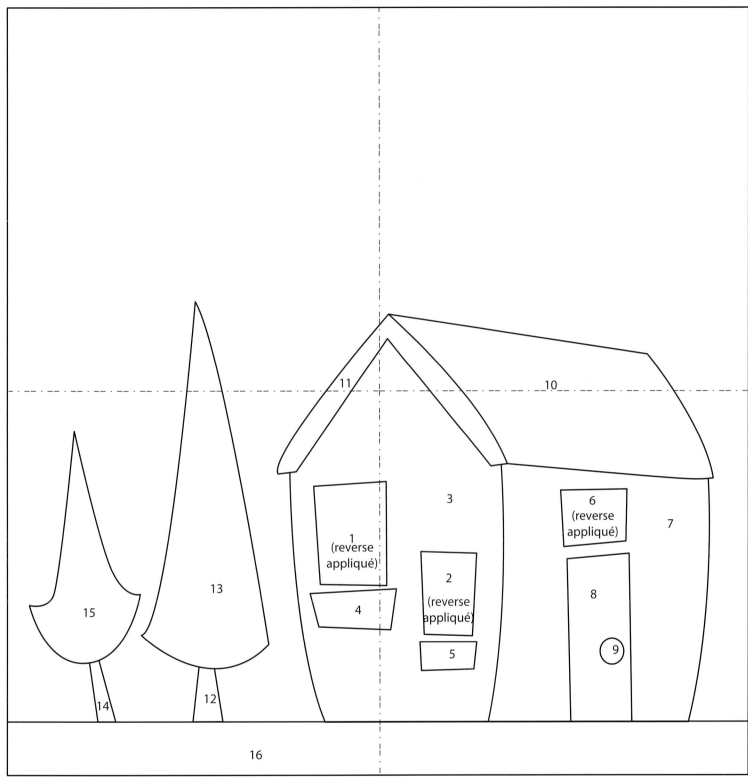

11

10

3

6
(reverse
appliqué)

7

1
(reverse
appliqué)

4

2
(reverse
appliqué)

8

5

9

13

15

14

12

16

Block 94

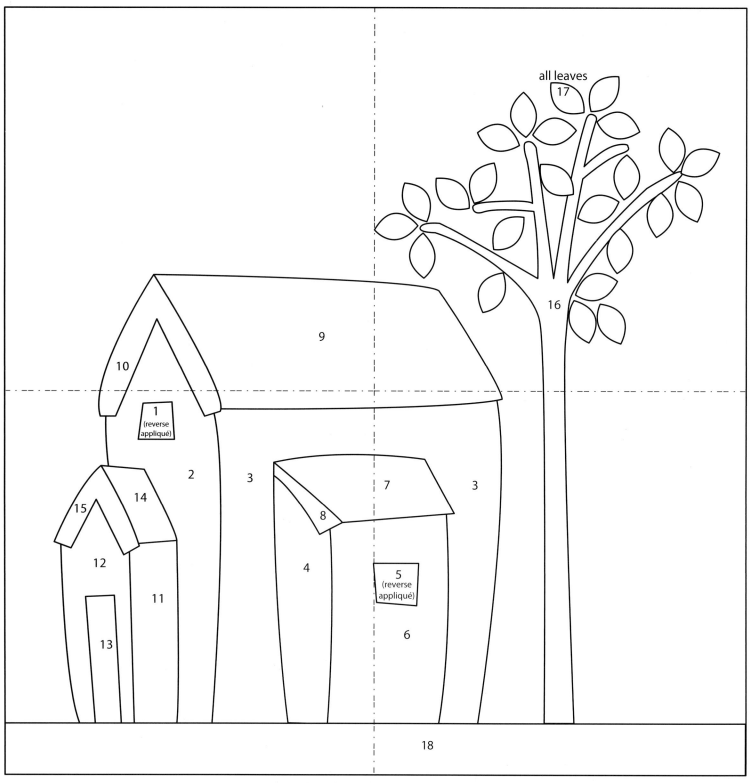

all leaves

17

16

9

10

1
(reverse
appliqué)

2

3

14

15

8

7

3

12

11

4

5
(reverse
appliqué)

13

6

18

Block 95

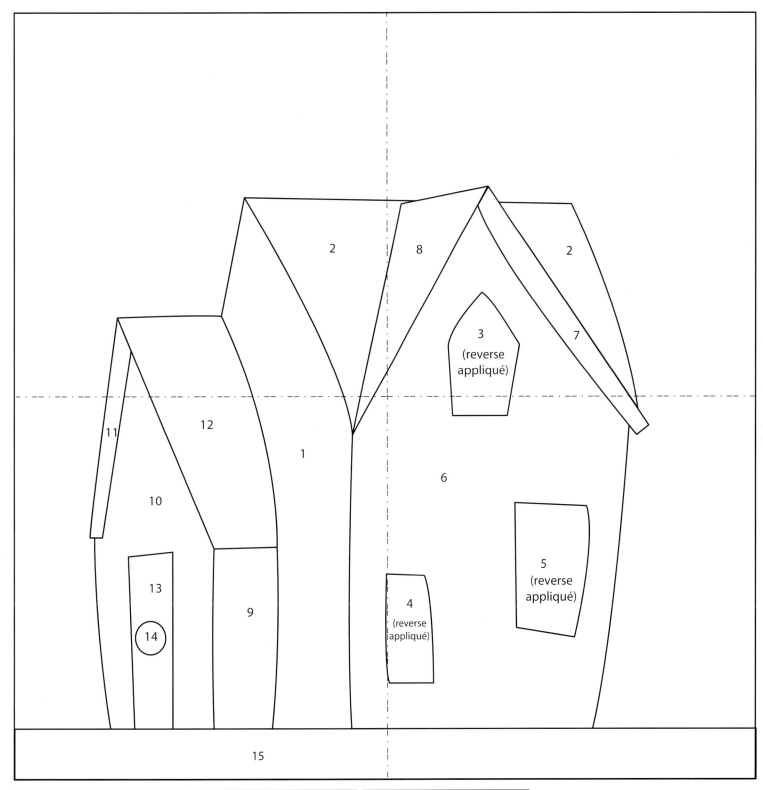

2

8

2

3
(reverse
appliqué)

7

11

12

1

6

10

5
(reverse
appliqué)

13

9

4
(reverse
appliqué)

14

15

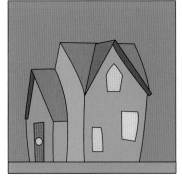
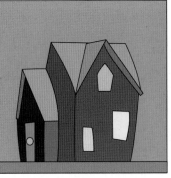

Block 96

all leaves
27

25 24 23

20 (reverse applique)

12 14 5 16 18

1 (reverse applique)

2 (reverse applique)

3 (reverse applique)

26

21 (reverse applique)

8 9 5 10 11

4 (reverse applique)

6

7

22 (reverse applique)

13 15 17 19

28

29

31 32 33 34 35 36 37 38 39 40 30 41 42 43 44 45 46 47

Block 97

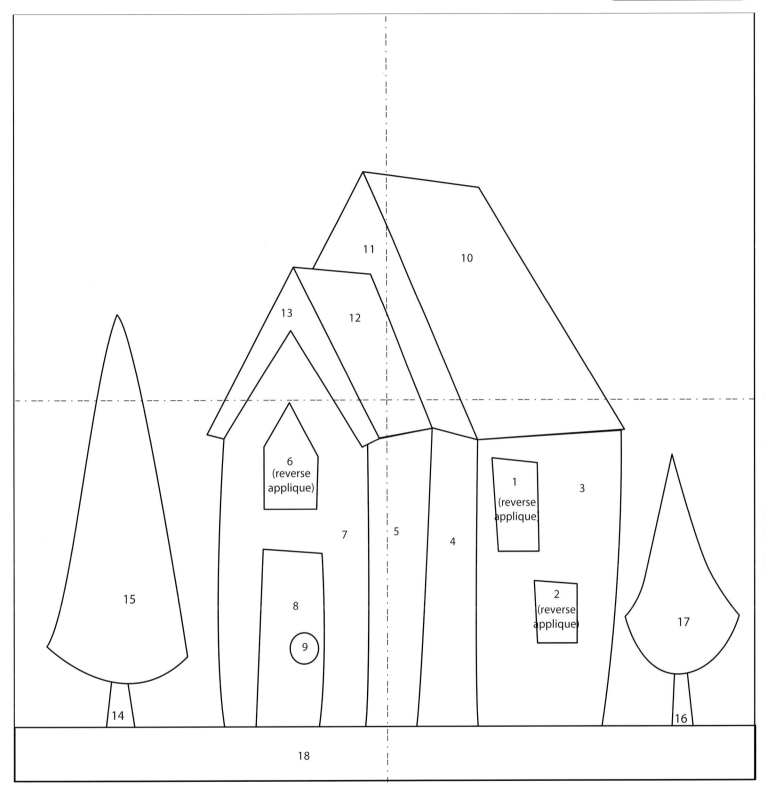

11

10

13

12

6
(reverse
applique)

1
(reverse
applique)

3

7

5

4

15

8

9

2
(reverse
applique)

17

14

16

18

Block 98

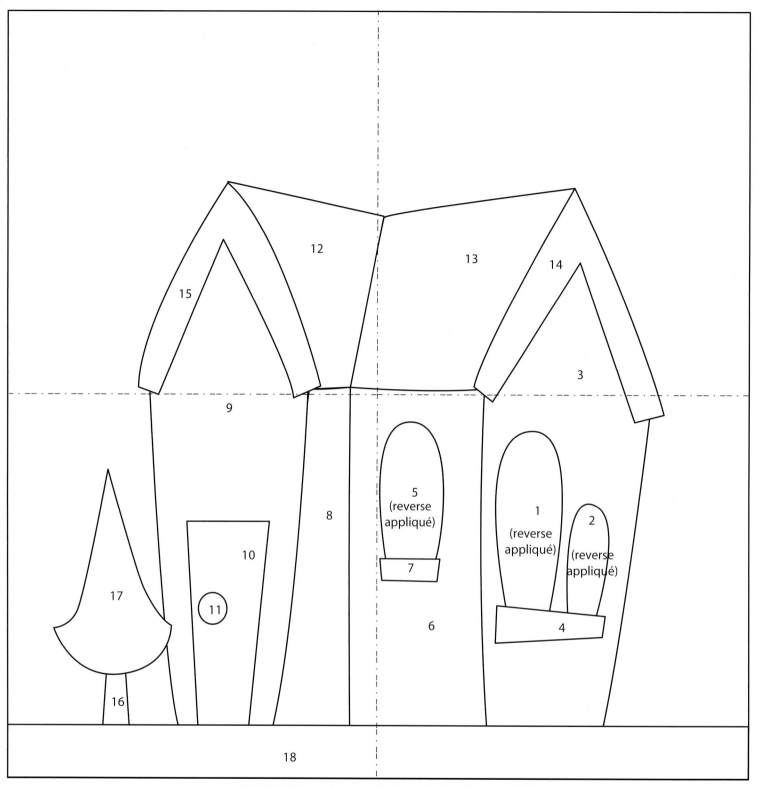

15

12

13

14

3

9

5
(reverse
appliqué)

1
(reverse
appliqué)

2
(reverse
appliqué)

8

10

7

11

6

4

17

16

18

Block 99

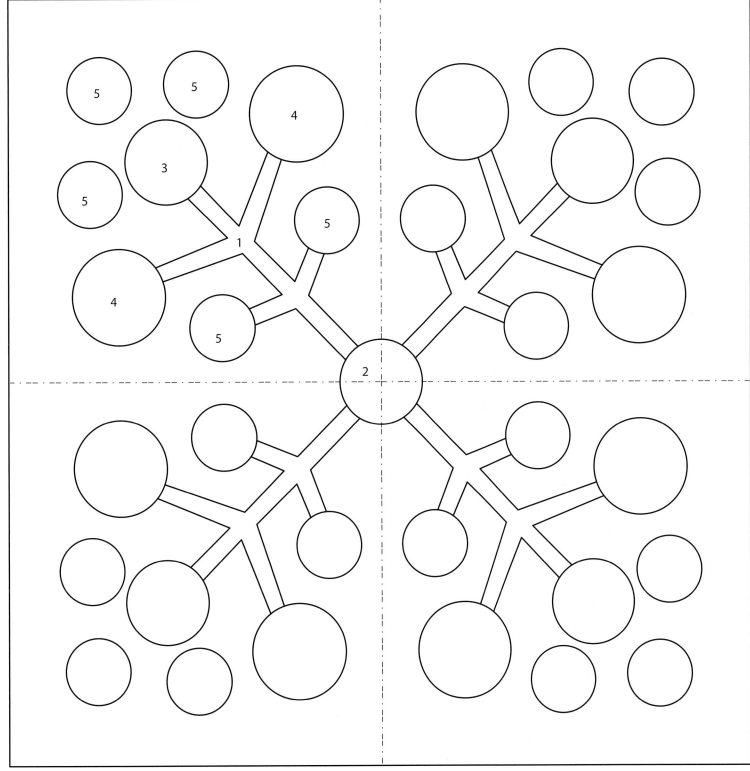

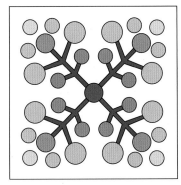 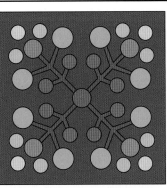 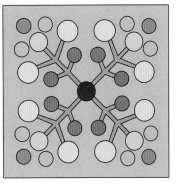

Block 100

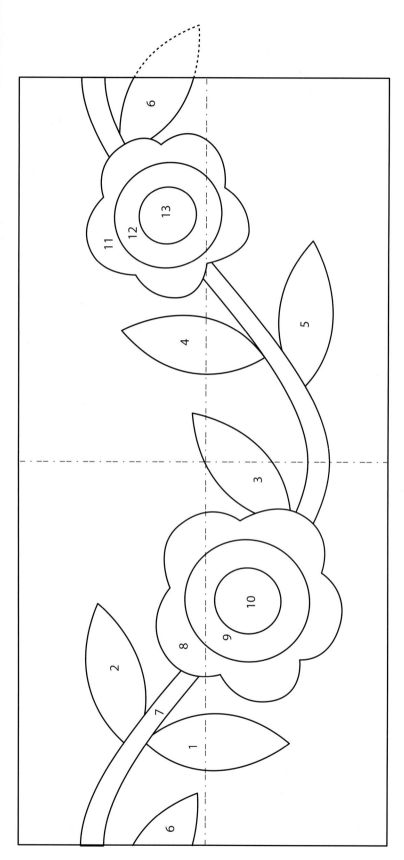

Border 101

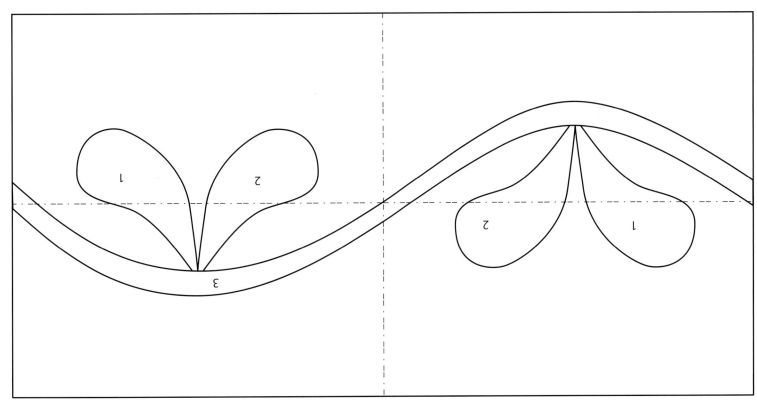

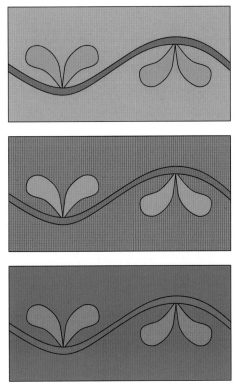

Border 102

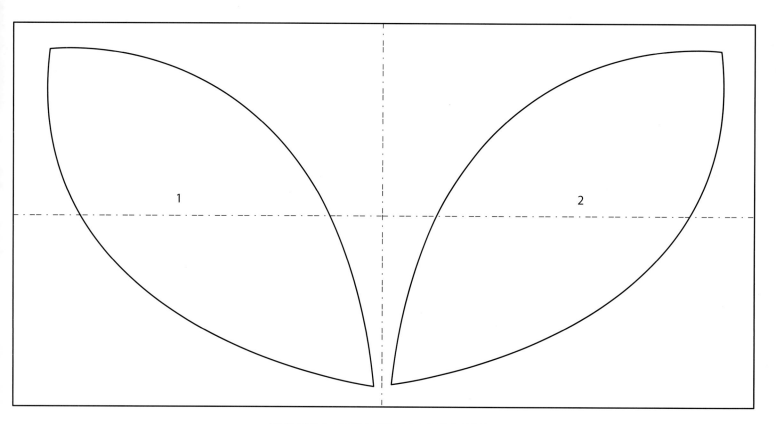

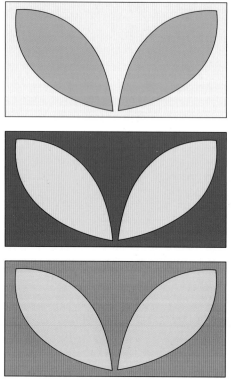

Border 103

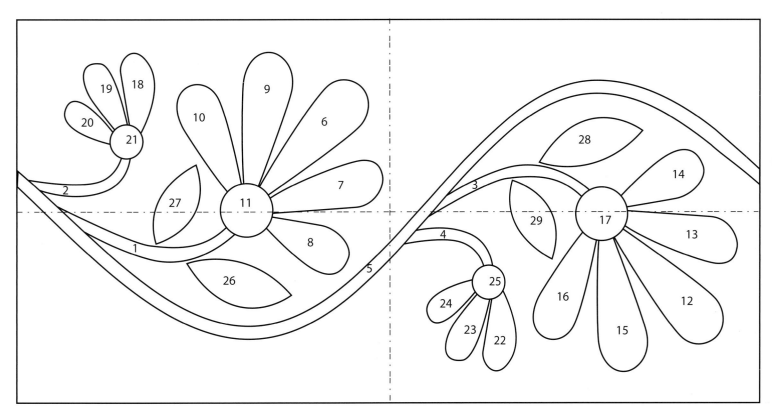

Border 104

About the Authors

Becky Goldsmith and Linda Jenkins met and became best friends forever at the Green Country Quilters Guild in Tulsa, OK. They started Piece O' Cake Designs in 1994 and, over the years, produced so many books and patterns that they have lost track of the number.

Linda retired from the business in 2014, but she is still appliquéing and giving Becky suggestions about what books and patterns ought to come next :-). Linda took an active part in putting this book together and made several of the quilts in the gallery.

Becky continues to write and publish new books and patterns under her own name and as Piece O' Cake. She teaches online and has a variety of online courses on Creative Spark. You can find Becky on Instagram @beckygoldsmith, and on Facebook at beckygoldsmith.pieceocake.

FIND PIECE O' CAKE ONLINE AT PIECEOCAKE.COM.

Becky Goldsmith

Linda Jenkins

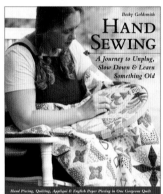

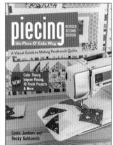